The Tale of the Coffee Bean Bandit

Written by Daniel Davis with Alma Golden

Illustrated by Sarah Hall

LUCIDBOOKS

DEDICATION

To my wonderful children, Reid, Annelise, Simon, Vivian, and Crosby, who never want to go to bed...but who probably need to.

To their beautiful mother who loves us all so freely. I love you, Joy.

To the God, who in all his wisdom, made us to need rest.

ONCE UPON A TIME

I am sure you have heard of some magical tales,
and I'm sure you have hoped some are true.

And I'm sure as you're snuggled up warm in your bed
You are hoping I'll tell one to you.

Do you see that young man
fast asleep on that bear?

Can you tell that he's had
quite a night?

This boy's name is Ben,
and the bear is his friend.

Shall I tell you what happened?
Alright.

One day just last week Ben was trying his luck

With a little exploring while playing with trucks.

And the last thing he grabbed right before he got stuck.

Was a shiny orange bag that was labeled "Starstrucks."

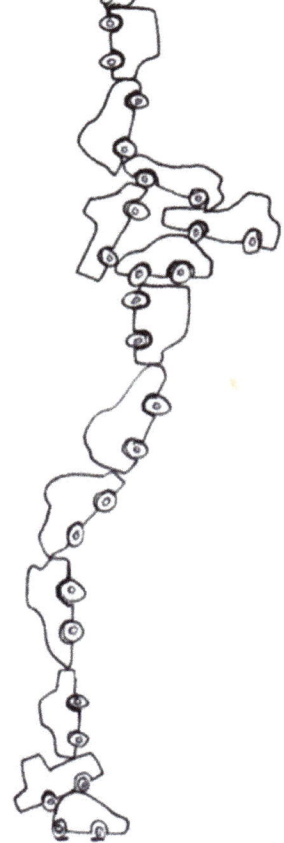

Ben's teacher had just read a story aloud

Of magical beans that grew up past the clouds.

He looked at these beans and he hoped with a sigh

I bet if I eat these, I'll sprout wings and fly!

Now children, I know, this is quite a big dream

But Ben, he was certain, and pulled out some beans

He chewed up a mouth-full – it tasted quite tragic.

But that's a small price for a food that is magic.

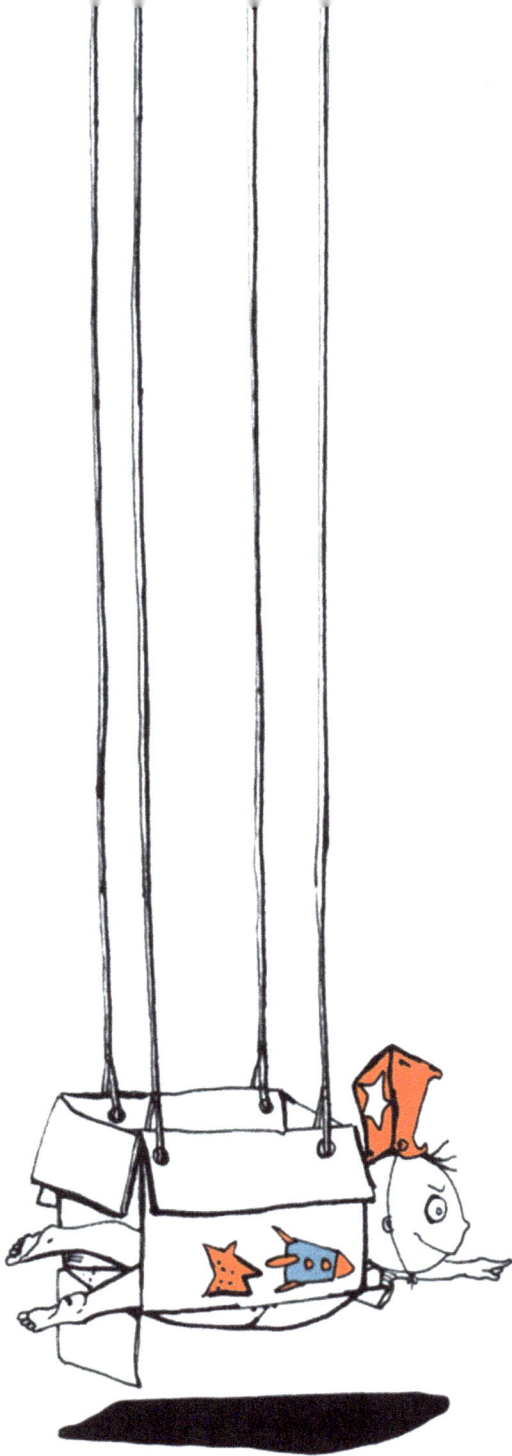

Ben's mind came alive as he played with his bear,

Imagining he would soon soar through the air.

He rummaged through boxes to pack a few things.

And felt on his shoulders to check for new wings.

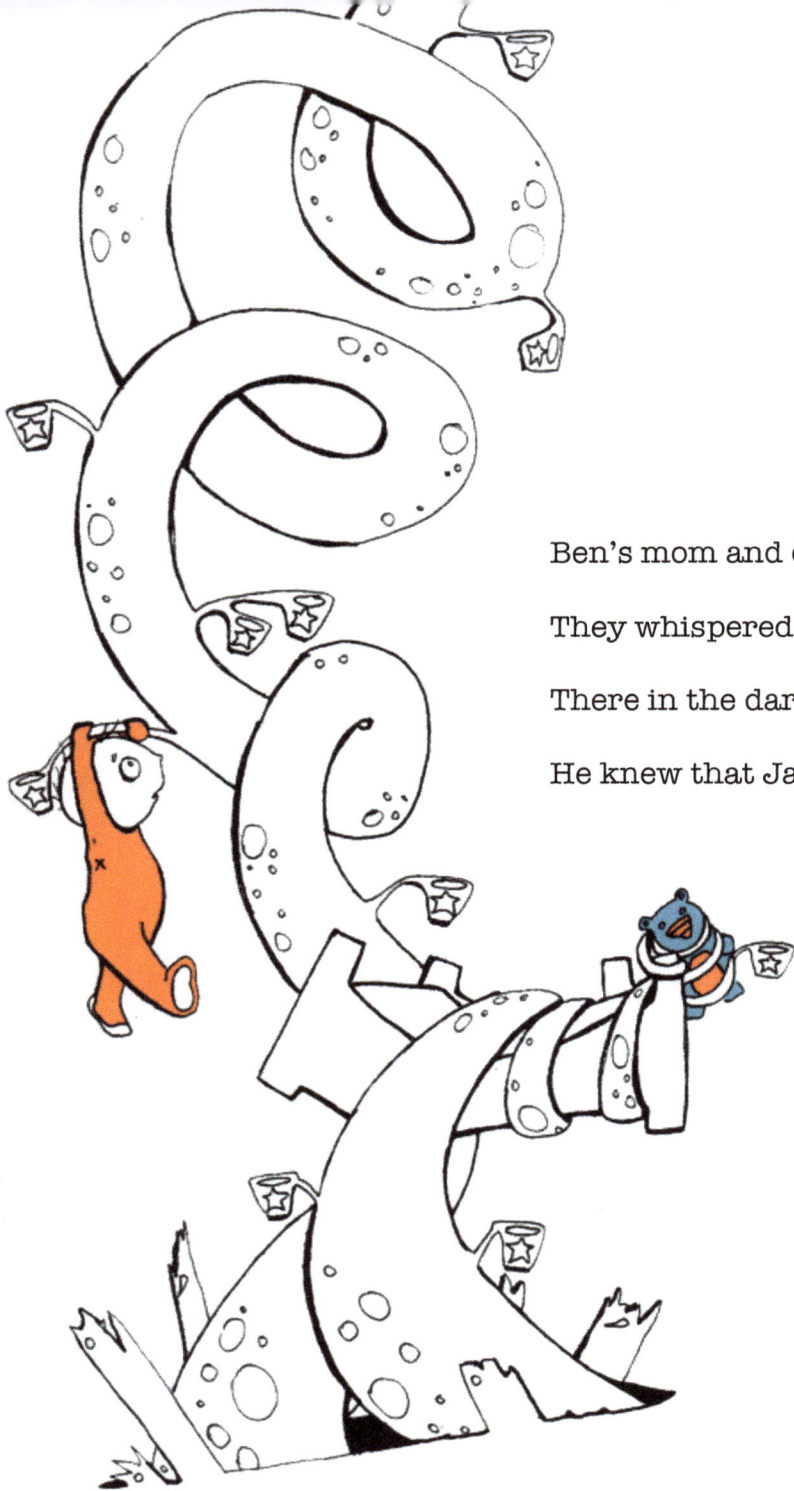

Ben's mom and dad tucked him into his bed.

They whispered a prayer and they both kissed his head.

There in the dark, he prepared for his flight.

He knew that Jack's beanstalk grew all in one night.

His eyes wouldn't shut, and he felt his heart beating.

Maybe, those beans are for planting...not eating.

He hopped out of bed, and he grabbed a few more.

He thought he'd stay up...just a minute...or four.

Staying up late is a lonely endeavor,

But Ben had a plan that was really quite clever.

Mommy, I miss you...

Dad...I want a drink!

I need to go potty.

There's a bear here!...I think.

Ben tried to sit still, and he tried to lay down.

He fidgeted watching the clock go around.

He couldn't stop dreaming up new games to play!

And he always remembered some great thing to say.

The later you're up you're more likely to find

The strangest ideas might just enter your mind.

Ben had to get up to show off to his folks

The tricks he had mastered and all his best jokes.

Ben's mom wondered what had got into her son.

And Ben noticed Dad was becoming less fun.

So there in his room with no hope of sleep,

The boy hunkered down in a tent made of sheets.

By midnight the boy had decided the beans

Would most likely not give him magical wings.

Now Ben was sure his unfortunate snack

Had given him strength, and he sensed an attack.

He imagined a foe hiding under his bed,

Or inside his closet, or out in the shed.

He knew that his powers were keeping him sharp.

He had never stayed up for this long after dark.

To those who've stayed up way past bedtime you know,

There's nothing to do, and the time moves so slow.

Then Ben came to grips with a terrible truth.

All that those beans did was hurt his sore tooth.

Instead of a flight or a fight, our young friend

Fell fast asleep right around 2AM.

The next day, the sun and the bus spun around,

And Ben was the crankiest bandit in town.

He hardly remembered the bus ride to school.

In class he awoke in a puddle of drool.

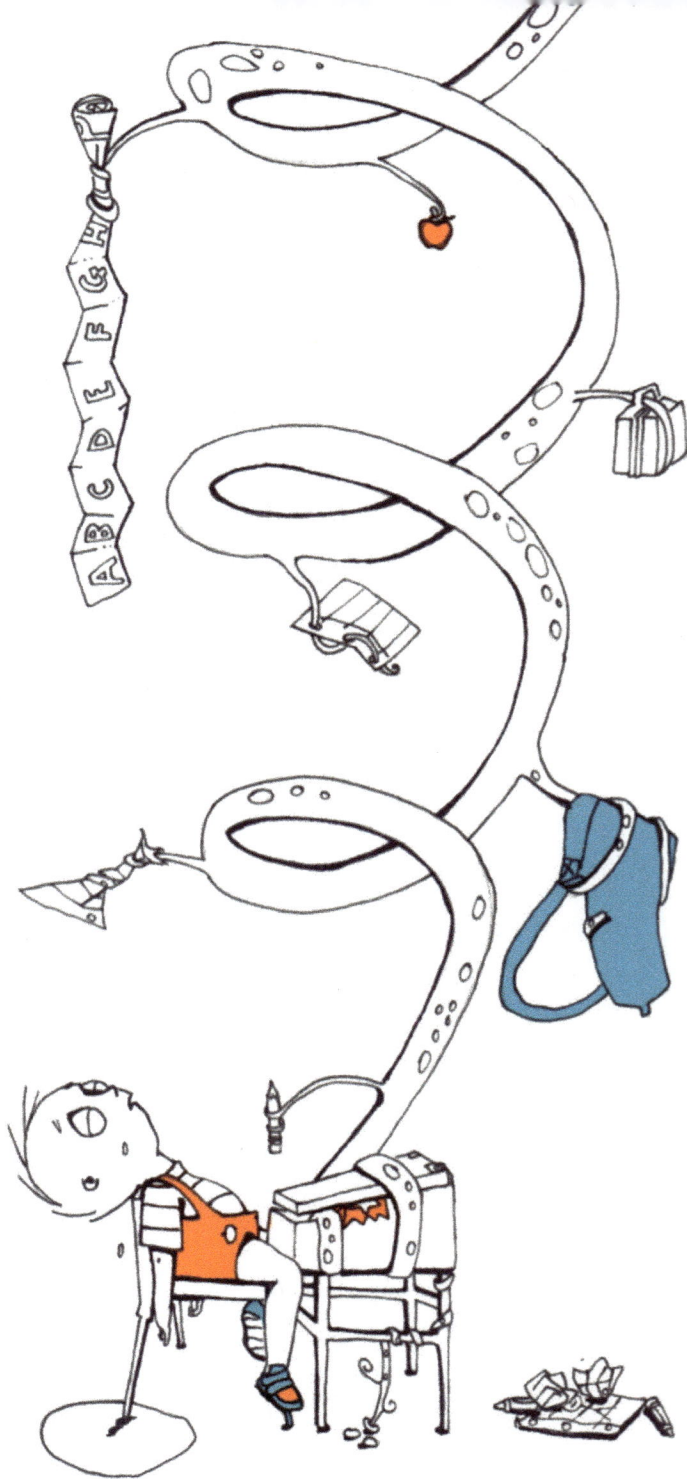

He began to think Starstrucks would need to explain

His long sleepless night, and the pain in his brain.

That night, he resolved to go back to his trucks,

And steer clear of the bag that was labeled "Starstrucks".

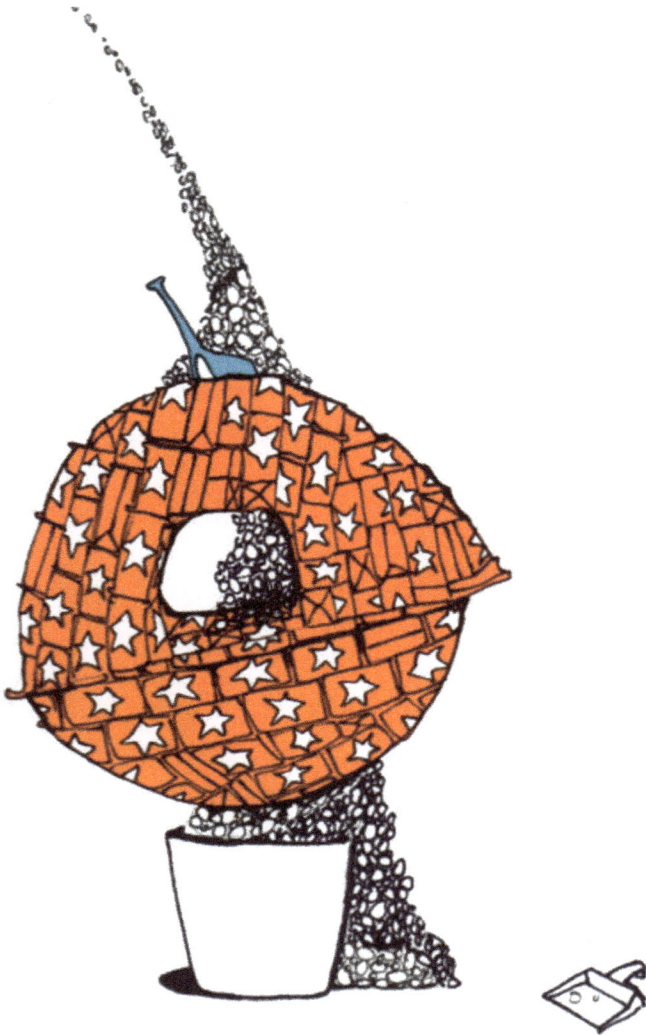

This ends the story of our Bean Bandit, Ben.

He ate up and stayed up, but never again.

Now I know that we talked of a magical tale,
And I know that is not what I've told.

But when counting your sheep for the magic of sleep,
Here's a comfort and promise to hold.

As you lay in your bed now, remember
Your body and mind need to rest.

Relax and breathe deep and then drift off to sleep.
You are more loved than you could have guessed.

HAPPILY EVER AFTER